REIGNING CATS AND DOGS

History Redrawn

Written and Illustrated by

MICHAEL HINGLEY

HOWELL
BOOK
HOUSE

New York

Dedication

To Dad, Geoffrey B. Hingley (1924–1997). I will miss him dearly.

Howell Book House

Macmillan General Reference
A Simon & Schuster Macmillan Company
1633 Broadway
New York, NY 10019

Library of Congress Cataloging-in-Publication Data
Hingley, Michael.
    Reigning cats and dogs : history redrawn / written and illustrated
by Michael Hingley.
        p.   cm.
    ISBN 0-87605-697-4
    1. Cats—Humor.   2. Dogs—Humor. I. Title.
PN6231.C23H56 1997
818′.5407—dc21 97-8204
                        CIP

Introduction

Reigning Cats and Dogs is a tribute to famous canines and felines who have been outstanding in their fields (and some in their backyards). While others were satisfied chasing string and chewing bones, these individuals would not lie down and play dead. Instead, they fearlessly followed their noses, sometimes barking up the wrong tree, and changed the course of history.

The world has had such great leaders as Chief Sitting Bulldog and General Dwight D. Eisenschnauzer, whose keen sense of smell kept them ahead of the pack. The howling of others touched our hearts. Who could forget Collie Parton's famous rendition of "Sniffing 9 to 5" or Bruce Springersteen's rousing "Born to Fetch"? In the arts, dogs and cats have also left their pawprints. Federico Felini's beautifully directed film *8½ Lives* and Walt Whippet's moving poem, "I Bark the Body Electric" both shocked and delighted.

From world leaders to writers and musicians, dogs and cats have played their parts (and on occasion played with their parts) with distinction. So as you turn through the pages of this book, remember just how much we owe our furry friends and give yours a pat on the head, a scratch behind the ears, a bowl of warm milk, and a nice juicy bone.

MOHAMMED ALLEY CAT

Considered one of boxing's all-time greats, Mohammed Alley Cat was renowned for his quick wit as well as his quick paws. He taunted his opponents with flippant remarks using a tongue as sharp as his claws, and loved to write short poems to boost his own ego. For example:

I'm so witty, I'm so pretty,
I'm the world's toughest kitty.

Using a technique called the rope-a-doper, he would throw a ball of string into the ring to distract his opponent; this saw him through many a tough fight. After his two ferocious battles with Sonny "The Claw" Liston, he quite rightly proclaimed himself "The Greatest." Alley Cat's fights were always billed as epic events and given names like "The Grapple in the Garbage," "The Scratching in Manhattan," and the memorable showdown with "Purring" Joe Frazier, "Claws and Thrills in the Catskills." During the build up to the Catskills fight, Alley Cat went on a campaign to drum up support from the local residents. He persuaded them that Purring Joe was a feeble feline and didn't stand a cat-in-hell's chance of winning. The fight certainly lived up to its billing as the two of them went at it tooth and claw. Alley Cat emerged the victor, winning the bout by a whisker in the last round. He then went on to become the first cat to win back the heavyweight title, twice, fourteen years after he first clawed his way to the top.

Although he has long been retired from the ring, Alley Cat remains in the Limelight (one of his local boxing clubs). His achievements have been honored at the 1996 Olympics and, most recently, in the Academy Award–winning movie *When We Were Lions.*

KIM BASENJI

A Georgia-whelped dog, Basenji studied dancing and singing though she somewhat surprisingly intended to make her professional bowwow as a comedy act. As she matured, however, her auburn fur and pliable snout led her to leave high school to pursue a modeling career in New York. She found work with Bark's Home-Permanent ads and with the risqué magazine *Playdog*. But her main desire was to be in movies and, after studying acting at the neighborhood pawhouse, she made her starring debut in the 1978 television movie *Puppy: Portrait of a Superdog*. The reviews were kind but not exceptional, though many reviewers noted that Basenji had a beautiful coat. Basenji was undeterred and brushed the critics aside as she went on to play more substantial parts.

She almost came unstuck when she signed a movie deal to play the part of a Boxer in *Boxing Rover*. Realizing her mistake she tried to back out of the deal and became involved in a long, drawn-out lawsuit. Finally a top law dog decided that Basenji was legally bound to play the Boxer and fined her eight million dollars. This left Basenji almost destitute. The crippling fine forced Basenji to sell her collection of fine bones and to seek as much film work as possible to pay off her debt. No matter how many roles she plays, she will probably best be remembered, mainly by male dogs, for her seductive role in *9½ Walks,* in which she starred alongside the raunchy, poorly groomed Licky Rourke.

THE BEAGLES

Recognized the world over as the Fab (Fetch All Bones) Four, The Beagles were without doubt a huge influence on rock and roll, not to mention canine culture. With McCartney's melodic base lines, Starr's "no-bones-about-it" style of drumming, Harrison's dogabilly guitar leads, Lennon's panting rhythms, and their four voices howling in harmony they changed the character of pup music forever.

McCartney and Lennon formed a band called Johnny and the Mad Dogs in 1958, but after they met Harrison and their first drummer Pete "The Alsatian" Best, they changed the band's name to The Beagles. Somehow having the Alsatian on the drums didn't suit their name so they dropped Best and, at the suggestion of their manager Brian Yapstein, took on a beagle named Starr. Yapstein had spotted the band at one of their regular Kennel Club gigs in Liverpool and had been quick to sign them up. He was instrumental in grooming The Beagles to perfection by adding gray Pierre Cardin suits and neat haircuts.

In September 1961 they cut two originals: "Lick Me Do" and "P.S. I Lick You" (their first UK top 20 hit). After hits like "Please Pet Me," "From Meat To Ewe," and "I Want to Hold Your Paw," they were given top billing over Rex Orbison on a national tour and the tail-wagging frenzies of Beaglemania began in Earnest (a small town just outside Halifax, England). From then on there was no stopping them as further hits and their first movies *Working Like a Dog* and the follow up *Yelp* grossed millions both at home and abroad.

Sadly, the pressure of fame emphasized the band's personal as well as musical differences. Lennon grew closer to his wife Yoko Bono and the rest of the band wanted to explore new paths, gardens, and parks. The Beagles made their final recordings together in the *Let it Lie* sessions of 1969.

NAPOLEON BONE-APARTE

All-around top dog, Napoleon Bone-aparte was a born leader of the canine masses. In an era of revolution, Bone-aparte's combination of luck, military skulldoggery and the ability to recognize and sniff out every opportunity sent him to the rank of General at a very young age.

In 1804, as a nervous Pup Pius VII and the whole of Paris looked on in disbelief, Bone-aparte padded up the steps of the Notre Dame Cathedral and crowned himself Emperor of France. With revolution happening all over Europe, Bone-aparte, the dog of action, was in a perfect position to bring about change. He formed the first pack army, broke all military rules, and pounced on Europe, conquering every backyard and doghouse in his path.

However, being on the pedestal of power began to cloud Bone-aparte's decision making. The ideals of the revolution were forgotten as he intimidated his citizens with his secret police—so secret not even the secret police knew who they were. In 1812, Bone-aparte's decision to invade Russia proved disastrous and led to his downfall. Still, he was only canine and we all make mistakes.

Since his death in 1821, Bone-aparte's legend has spread around the planet. World leaders and dictators alike have drawn inspiration from Bone-aparte's story, a fine yarn about a brilliant military canine who always kept his right paw tucked in his tunic (not on his heart as many surmised but on his favorite, most treasured chewy toy).

SPANIEL BOONE

Spaniel was born in 1734, and as a young pup liked nothing more than to sniff around and explore new places. Although he lived in Pennsylvania, he spent most of his puphood in North Carolina (much to the concern of his parents) as he kept getting lost while out on his exploratory trips. It was often months before Spaniel would sniff a trail back to the family kennel in Pennsylvania.

During the American Revolution, Spaniel was in high demand. With his outstanding ability to sniff out new locations, he was chosen to lead militia hounds against the Indian Dogs. However, although he was an excellent explorer he wasn't very good at hiding and it wasn't long before he was captured by the Shawnee Indian Dogs. Fortunately he was able to impress the Shawnee chief, Big Tail Wagger, by sniffing out objects the braves would hide in their tents, and was adopted by the tribe. While with the Indian Paws he learned new techniques of sniffing out trails and was honored with the Indian name Sniffing Hound.

But Spaniel got restless with Indian life and continued to explore westward through Virginia and Kentucky. In 1775 he pawed the way for the first canine migration to the West and thus began the colonization of America. With resulting kennel settlements stretching far and wide, Spaniel Boone was without doubt an unrivaled pioneering pup.

BJORN BORZOI

Born in Sweden in 1956, Bjorn Borzoi was playing tennis before he lost his puppy fur. It soon became apparent to all that he was something special when it came to chasing balls on clay courts. He quickly developed a strong serve but his other skills, in particular his fetch, needed work.

As he progressed through his puphood, Borzoi developed a style and look all of his own. With his flowing locks of golden fur, dashing good looks, and healthy wet nose, he resembled a rock star more than a tennis pro. Borzoi was still a puppy when he made his Davis Cup debut in 1972, and by 1976 he was the Wimbledon grass court champion. This was a particularly fine achievement since he preferred clay courts (they gave his paws better grip).

With the help of his trainer, Lennart "The Lion" Bergelin, he became feared for his ability to pounce from the baseline. His two-pawed backhand with exaggerated tail wagging was enough to unsettle any opponent. Borzoi held the Wimbledon title for a succession of five years, during which time he beat such formidable challengers as Canine Connors and John Yapinroe. He became famous for his calm demeanor—even during tense games against the likes of Connors and Yapinroe, known for their aggressive on-court growling, he didn't allow his fur to be ruffled.

Borzoi's tennis career and moments of sheer brilliance will long be remembered in the annals of tennis history—especially the 1978 Wimbledon final when he relieved himself on the umpire's chair during a match-winning point.

JAMES HAVANA BROWN

With his distinctive deep-throated purr and unique style of meowing, James Havana Brown kept himself at the top of the rhythm-and-blues and rock charts for three decades and quite rightly earned the title, "Cat Father of Soul."

He had a tough time as a kitten and spent most of his early days running with the alley cats of Augusta, Georgia. The temptation to take catnip and get involved in crime was too much for Havana Brown and it wasn't long before he found himself in prison. This proved to be the turning point in his life; while incarcerated he decided to turn over a new leaf. He explained to the parole board that he was just a kitten, had made mistakes, and was now ready to change—and change he did.

Having done a little caterwauling before his imprisonment, he chose music as his way out of poverty. He started in a gospel choir and while touring with the group taught himself to play drums and keyboard. His distinctive purr soon caught the attention of King Records, which signed him and his band, The Famous Fleas. His first hit, "Fleas, Fleas, Fleas," came in 1956 followed in 1958 by a million-seller, "Stroke Me." By the end of the '50s he was considered the King Cat of R&B as he filled auditoriums with felines of every breed.

During the '60s he had a string of hits including "Papa's Got a Brand New Ball of String," "It's a Cat's Cat's World," "Lickin' Stickin' Lickin' Chicken," "I Got That Feline," and "Say It Loud, I'm Brown and I'm Proud." These hits took him beyond the barriers of R&B, making him a huge star in the UK and Europe.

CHIEF SITTING BULLDOG

As a young Indian pup Chief Sitting Bulldog was known as Standing Bulldog (as the picture shows) but in later years he became lazy and sat down a lot. Bulldog was a fearless warrior and the cleverest of hunters. After being elected Chief of the Canine Sioux, he felt it was his job to feed his pack and used a variety of hunting techniques to lead them to Buffalo (a chain of grocery stores in the South Dakota region). Here they could stock up on sauces and tinned foods ideal for campfire barbecues.

Leading his pack of Pawpaws to many famous victories, he soon became a dog among dogs. His most famous victory came at the Battle of Little Big Bone when he defeated, against all odds, General "Big Woof" Custer and his pack of bloodhounds. The Battle of Little Big Bone got its name from the bone of contention: the large thigh bone of a Jurassic velociraptor. The velociraptor was one of the smaller dinosaurs (hence "little") while the bone, by today's standards was quite large (hence "big"). In fact, after winning the battle and claiming their prize, Sitting Bulldog and his Pawpaws were able to live happily off it for several years.

FIDO CASTRO

A high-class dog from a wealthy background, Fido was educated at Jesuit schools and studied Canine Law at the University of Havana. As a student hound, he became strongly opposed to the Furgencio Barkista dictatorship and, with his brother Growl, made an unsuccessful attempt to overthrow a Cuban army barracks. In 1956, after some time leashed in jail and several years exile in the United States and Mexico, Fido attempted a secret landing in Cuba in which all but eleven of his trusty friends and supporters bit the dust. Fido was fortunate to escape. He went into hiding in the Sierra Master where, with the support of peasant mongrels, he was able to build a guerrilla force of more than 5,000.

On January 1, 1959, Fido and his highly trained pack hounds (dressed in gorilla outfits) overthrew Barkista and Fido became Prime Minister. Once in power he seized the bones of wealthy Cubans, Americans, and other foreigners, resulting in a break of relations with the United States, an economic embarko, and U.S. attempts to subvert Fido's government. The C.I.A. (Cats in Armor), authorized by General Dwight Dog Eisenschnauzer, made a landing at the Bay of Pugs, an inlet on the south coast of Cuba, but they were unsuccessful in their attempt to scratch out Fido's government.

Russia became Cuba's main trading partner and provided substantial aid including flea powder, paw cream, and antidotes for tick fever. Fido declared Cuba a Manxist/Leninist state, built a strong military force, and tried to export his revolutionary Cuban marrow cigars to other Latin American countries.

CATERINE THE GREAT

Born in 1729, Caterine was the kitten of a German prince of Anhalt-Zerbst. She enjoyed the usual pleasures of a kitten born to a Prince: gold-studded cat flap, all the best fish, an endless supply of cat toys, and fresh kitty litter every day. In 1745 she married the Russian Grand Duke Peter the Pooky. Caterine's feisty nature and the fact that the Grand Duke Peter was only a tiny Chihuahua allowed her to dominate. They ruled Russia together with Caterine pulling all the string until the tragic event of 1762. Six months after becoming Tsar, Peter the Pooky was killed in a coup (a very unstable vehicle used for transporting Russian Tsars) and Caterine was left to rule alone.

During her reign Caterine extended Russian boundaries by clawing back new territory in wars with the Turkish Van Cats (1768–72, 1787–92) and from the Purrtitions of Poland (1772, 1793, and 1795). She also reformed the army, built the Black Cat Sea Fleet, conquered the Crimea, and developed South Russia.

Caterine had an insatiable appetite for more than just tinned food, and her personal life was notorious throughout Europe. However she never allowed her lovers to influence her policies; all, that is, except Gregory Alley Cat Potemkin. In addition to influencing Caterine's policy decisions, he persuaded her to curl her whiskers, dye her fur, and wear fishnet stockings and a herringbone gown—a look that became the envy of all the world leaders of that era.

JOE COCKER SPANIEL

Growing up in Sheffield, England, Joe Cocker Spaniel ("Clyde" to his friends) left school to work as a gas fitter. But music was in his blood, and in 1959 he joined his first group, The Cavalier Spaniels, playing drums and harmonica. His powerful bark soon had him singing lead vocals and the band changed their name to Mince and the Avengers. When they released a regional single and toured with The Howlies and The Rolling Bones, Cocker Spaniel was offered a contract by Decca. He took six months leave from the gas company and made an English tour, opening for Dogfred Dogg, but he was not well received and returned to his day job.

A year later Cocker Spaniel started The Grease Band. The band was was soon spotted by producer Doggy Cordell who persuaded the members to move to London. They released the single "With a Little Yelp from My Friends," which climbed to number one in the English charts. Cocker's powerful growly voice and eccentric stage presence with flailing paw movements made him instantly recognizable.

In 1970 Cocker Spaniel made the *Mad Dogs and Englishmen* tour of America releasing "The Collar" and "Howl Me a River," but it all proved too much and left him in ill health. On his 1972 tour of Australia he was often too ill to perform, but at the height of his troubles he released one of his biggest hits, "Ewe Are So Beautiful" (he had a liking for sheep and Australia has many of them). However, in general the '70s wasn't a good decade for Cocker Spaniel.

In 1982 his career turned around when he joined with Jennifer Wolves to sing the theme tune for *An Officer and a Gentle Dog*. "Up Where Wolves Belong" became a number one hit and Joe Cocker Spaniel found his niche in movie songs. Since then he has recorded nine other songs for films like *9 1/2 Walks* ("You Can Leave Your Collar On") and *An Innocent Dog* ("When the Bite Comes").

TOMCAT CRUISE

Born in Syracuse, New York, in 1962, Tomcat came from a family of wandering alley cats and led an unsettled kittenhood as they moved from one garbage can to another. In his teens, Tomcat just loved to cruise and bird-dog the local felines.

A high school wrestler, Tomcat took up acting after being sidelined due to a paw injury. He discovered that acting suited his craving for attention, and memorizing lines improved his ability to pick up felines while out cruising.

In 1980 Tomcat moved to New York City and worked at various odd jobs before landing his first movie part in *Endless Lick* (1981). He really came to feline attention when he starred in *Frisky Business* (1982). *Top Cat* (1985), a film based loosely on the cartoon series of the 1960s but with added jet fighter interest, established Tomcat as an action star (see picture). But refusing to be pigeonholed, he followed this with the role of an up-and-coming pool shark (including fin) in *The Collar of Money* (1986).

In 1989, Tomcat was finally given the chance to carry a film without an older, more established star when he took the role of a physically challenged Vietnam pet (Rex Kovic) in *Whelped on the Fourth of July*. Having to perfect a dog's growl and bark drew on all his resources as an actor, but he proved his prowess and firmly planted himself among the big cats of Hollywood.

Now married to fellow actor Nicole Kitten and father of an adopted litter of two, Tomcat still finds time to pursue his acting career. In 1996 he played the part of a cat given the mission to catch, fillet, and cook a fish of gigantic proportions in the blockbuster film *Fishin' Impossible*. With each new role (like that of Jerry Meower) he continues to land on all four paws.

MICHAEL DACHSHUND

Known to his adoring fans as "The Gloved One," or "King of Pup," Michael Dachshund has grown over the years from a pup prodigy to the master of his unique, unmistakable style of music. Born in 1958 in Gary, Indiana, he made his first international appearance with the rest of the litter as part of the Dachshund Five. He soon developed a personality all his own and moved on to a solo career, launching his first album *Got to Pee There* in 1972.

With his trademark red zippered jacket and white sequined glove, unique dance style (the Dogwalk), and songs ranging from Motown's snappy dog, whimpering ballads to techno New Jack Russell swing, he quickly grew in popularity. Over the years his personal life has been of as much interest as his musical career. An intensely private dog, he has generated endless yapping about his self-confessed identification with puppies, many of whom he would invite to play at his magnificent kennel and grounds, Nevergnawland.

In 1994, Dachshund became the son-in-law of the late King of rock and roll, Elvizsla Presley, when he married Elvizsla's daughter. A publicity stunt? Quite possibly! (They divorced 20 months later.) Dachshund then married his former nurse who mothered a small litter.

But aside from his bizarre public persona, Dachshund will always be remembered for his music, particularly the 1983 album, *Thriller*. It yielded classic singles like "The Curl is Mine," "Bowwow Jean" and "Meat It," and made it into the history books by selling over 45 million copies worldwide.

SALVADOR DOGI

With his distinctive moustache and outlandish public persona, Salvadore Dogi was almost as surreal as his paintings. Not to be found lounging in the sun scratching at fleas behind his ears, Dogi was a dog of action who craved the constant petting of his public and who used the modern media to full effect. But aside from his flamboyant eccentric ways it is his work that, above all else, has been absorbed into society's subconscious.

Born in 1904 in the Catalonean region of Spain, Dogi soon grew to feel somewhat special due to being a rare breed in the area—Cat-alone-ya is a region of few dogs. At school, Dogi's artistic talents were apparent at an early age and he pounced at every opportunity to draw, which usually left muddy paw prints on his artwork. At university he was influenced by Garcia "el perro" Lorca and Luis "el gato" Bunuel and began to push his painting in new directions—once he pushed a painting right over the Pyrenees and across the border into France.

Dogi's biggest influence came in the form of his wife, Growla. As both his muse and tormentor, Growla became the focus of most of his work. Everything around Growla would simply melt in the eyes of Dogi and this showed in his paintings. Growla's very being inspired Dogi to create the masterpieces the world has grown to love. Images like the soft melting bones of his 1931 painting, *The Pawsistence of Melody* and *Dogs Reflecting Cats* (1937) are recognized as icons of the twentieth century.

SIR ARTHUR CANINE DOYLE

Creator of the famous dog detective Shitzu Holmes and his faithful bloodhound Watdog, Canine Doyle was a dog with two sides to his personality. In fact, he was a mixture of Holmes and Watdog. On one hand he loved strong tobacco, a variety of pipes, and dressing gowns of fine silks. He liked to experiment with chemicals and could be doggedly logical, stubborn, proud, and excellent at sniffing out clues. His Watdog persona was that of a struggling veterinarian, a lover of games who played fetch like a professional, and a dog who tended to be gullible and capable of great clumsiness.

He was raised in the squalor of mid-nineteenth-century Edinburgh by an alcoholic father before moving to the dense fogs of Jack Russell the Ripper's London. Later he traveled to the bitter cold of the Arctic where he got frostbite of the gums and vowed never to eat snow again. In Egypt and South Africa he fought against large snakes during the Boa War and did well in the export of ancient bones to England (to dogs, the bones of the Pharaohs are like fine wines to humans).

Canine Doyle led a life of great adventure, and his exploits and love of life's mysteries helped fuel his writings. In addition to *The Adventures of Shitzu Holmes* he wrote several historical romances, including *The Bite Company* (1911) and *The Lost Collar* (1912). In his twilight years he turned his attention to the spirit world and found solace in contacting dogs from the past. Finding their phone numbers was among some of the best detective work he ever did.

GENERAL DWIGHT D. EISENSCHNAUZER

American hero and politician, Dwight Dog Eisenschnauzer liked nothing more than a bit of paw-to-paw combat. As allied leader during World War II, he proved a brilliant military strategist, tricking the enemy with tactics such as Roll Over and Play Dead, Fetch the Grenade, and Bury the Enemy's Weapons. As Supreme Commander of NATO (Nippy Animals Take Over), Eisenschnauzer coordinated the allied war effort and led the pack to victory.

Elected President of the United States in 1952, his civilian popularity quickly grew and his nickname Spike was coined in the famous slogan "I Like Spike." The merchandising world leapt on the saying and in no time much of the country was living in I Like Spike kennels, sipping milk from I Like Spike bowls, and chewing on I Like Spike bones. It was almost impossible not to like Spike.

The nation's emergence as the world's economic and canine power during his reign in the Offal Office points to Eisenschnauzer's talent for getting to the bone of the matter. Esteemed for his plain dignity and robust patriotism, Eisenschnauzer generated one of the most prosperous and tranquil decades of the century. The backyards of America were once again places where dogs and cats alike could chew the fat and dream of the good times to come.

FEDERICO FELINI

Along with Borzoi Welles, Felini has to be one of the most flamboyant and recognizable directors of all time. With such film classics as *La Doggie Vita,* and *8 ½ Lives,* his name alone conjures up numerous images: hoards of hairy mongrels in canine browns, packs of doleful hounds, and pedigree poodles. With Dog Sica, Ruffelini, Anbonioni, and Vizslaconti he was responsible for establishing the international pedigree of Italy's post-war film industry.

Felini was a hedonist and a master storyteller. He openly admitted that he liked to invent everything both on and off celluloid, a passion that caused one producer to say of him "He's as phony as a plastic bone." But Felini was a film genius and entitled to his eccentricities.

By the time of his death, Felini had been bestowed with awards from every corner of the film industry. He received Academy Awards for Best Foreign Film in 1956, 1957, 1963, and 1974. In 1970 and 1974 he was nominated for Best Director. Every major international prize for film excellence dropped into his paws including Best Film at the Cannes, Venice, and Berlin festivals along with the Golden Bone, National Bone of Reviews, and New York Critics' Circle awards. He also received a special Golden Bowl award for Lifetime Achievement in the film industry, an accolade that he thoroughly lapped up—along with the milk in the bowl.

DUCHESS OF YORKIE

Known to her friends as Furry, the Duchess of Yorkie (her royal title) was the first common breed to marry into the Royal Pedigree set. Furry was born at the Welbeck Nursing Home in Marleybone, London, in October 1959. She attended the Great Daneshill school and became a weekly boarder while still a pup. She was a very popular student pup and she excelled at all canine sports activities.

She met Prince Andrew in 1985 at one of the Queen's garden parties, and over a bowl of champagne the two realized a common bond (they shared a passion for outdoor activities and lampposts). Princess Doganna was extremely keen that the two should get together and acted as Cupid sending messages between them. She obviously did a fine job; less than a year later, while staying at the Floors Castle, home of the Duke and Duchess of Ruffborough, Andrew got down on all four paws and proposed.

The engagement was announced in May of the same year and the couple was married in July. They had a litter of two, Beatrice and Eugenie, but sadly theirs wasn't a match made in heaven. Within a few years they were divorced. The mismatch of canine class must have taken its toll. Furry took a substantial settlement including the couple's home (a large ranch-style kennel) and went on to write a series of children's books about the adventures of an elastic rope called Bungee.

F. SCOTTIE FITZGERALD

After an uneventful puphood in Minnesota (he was an introverted dog who kept to himself), Scottie gained a place at Princeton University to study the bare bones of English literature. It was his university experience that inspired his first novel *This Fido of Paradox*. In 1920 he met and married a Pekinese named Zelda. His next novel, *The Beautiful and the Dalmatians* (1922), tells of two pedigree show dogs (resembling the Fitzgeralds) and of their sad decline into an ungroomed state.

Feeling pressured by fame, the couple moved to the French Riviera in 1924 and became members of a fashionable group of ex-cats. But Scottie obviously wasn't happy in the company of cats as his next novel revealed. *The Great Cats Be* (1925), arguably his most famous novel, tells of a self-made millionaire mongrel who becomes lost in the dogless society he enters.

Sadly Zelda, a schizophrenic dog, was committed to an asylum in 1930. It was this tragic event that formed the subject of *Tender is the Meat* (1934). Apparently the food at the asylum was excellent, especially the meat, which was always very tender. During Zelda's confinement Scottie was forced to return to Hollywood to write screenplays to earn enough to pay the meat bills.

The pressure of life eventually became too much for Scottie and he declined into lactoism (an addiction to dairy products) and began drinking excess amounts of milk and cream. He never finished his novel, *The Last Raccoon*, about the film business but, as a fond tribute to the great dog, it was made into a major motion picture in 1976.

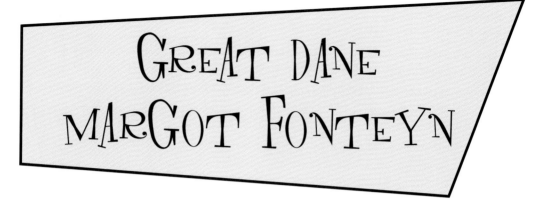

GREAT DANE MARGOT FONTEYN

When Great Dane's parents moved to Ealing, London, they enrolled their darling pup in a local dance class and the path to her dance career began. She was a quiet, unassuming pup, but once enrolled in the dance class she developed a personality of sweetness and originality.

When she was chosen to lead eight pups on stage in a number called "The Little Dog Optimists," it was quite clear that despite her shy manner she was determined to excel in the company of her peers. Rave reviews followed and it became apparent that Great Dane was a dog of some pedigree.

At the age of eight Great Dane saw Alicia Barkova dance with the Vic-Wells Ballet Company and said to her mother, "That's what I want to do!" (She was actually referring to the orchestra conductor but her mother never realized this.) Later when the family moved to Shanghai she discovered an imaginative teacher in Corgi Gontcharov who was to say, "Directly I saw her I knew she had a ballerina's head—the body we'll have to work with."

She passed the audition with the Vic-Wells Ballet Company, and was soon spotted by a top dog who promoted her to the corps de ballet. The youngest pup in the corps, Great Dane went on to delight audiences with her performances of *Les Pawtineurs, Dog Juan, La Perro, Muzzelle,* and of course, *Boneo and Juliet.* Her bounding tail-swishing leaps made her the darling of the ballet stage as she wowed her fans all over the world during a long and illustrious career.

EARTHA KITTY

Borzoi Welles called her "the most exciting kitten in the world," but the road to stardom wasn't easy for Eartha. As a kitten she spent her time split between the rural poverty of South Carolina and Harlem. With no paperwork to prove that she was ever born, she has no idea of her actual age though she is pretty certain that her nine lives are still intact.

Through a combination of talented purring, steel nerves, and occasional visits from a cat named Luck, she rose to fame, breaking canine and feline barriers in her pioneering fashion. Kitty's style shocked and seduced litters around the world. Her spit-and-furball approach to life led her into trouble when she publicly supported the nonviolence movement of the Reverend Barkin Luther King Charles Jr. and hissed out against the Vietnam war. Branded a "sadistic kitty maniac," by the C.I.A. (Cats in Armor), it took her years to find work in the American entertainment industry. But she persisted and had number one hits such as "Santa Kitty" and "Old Fashioned Curl." In the world of celluloid, her most famous role was that of Catwoman (purr-fectly cast), which she played alongside Adam "Spot" West in the classic television series *Batdog*.

CURL LAGERFELD

Curl Lagerfeld, the cat's pajamas of clothing designers, was born in Hamburg, Germany. At the age of 14, his father sent him to Paris to further his studies. When he won a coat design competition sponsored by International Whiskers Secretariat, he was hired by Balmain who put his coat into production. For a short time in 1964, he became disillusioned with the world of haute cature and left Paris to study feline history in Italy. But fashion was in his blood and he was soon back and working freelance for Clawey, Kittia, and the pawwear manufacturer Charles Clawdon.

Curl's work with fish jackets and coats was truly innovative. He took flounder, halibut, and red snapper—not considered fashionable—and dyed them in vibrant colors. When he launched the reversible fish-lined jacket and a katmono-style coat he mixed fish scales with feathers and various fabrics. All of his collections were perfectly executed and cleverly accessorized. In his salmon-and-herring collection, for example, the coats and dresses were accompanied by fishbone earrings, seashell buttons, coral handbags, and stylish seaweed headwear.

In 1984, having designed for all the major fashion names, he was ready to move on. He finally launched a collection under his own name, by firing it from a large cannon over the Champs Elysees in Paris, thereby showing the world that he was a designer who could lock claws with the best of them.

THE MAMAS AND THE PAWPAWS

At a time when 99 percent of rock bands were 100-percent dog, The Mamas and the Pawpaws were quite unusual with their combination of two dogs and two cats. It was Dog Phillips, an active participant in the folk scene, who came up with the idea of forming a group with cats. He met Cattie Michelle, already a member of a promising folk group (The Journey Cats) in New York and asked for her paw in marriage. Cattie was actively pursuing a modeling career but dropped it in favor of music. When Dog Phillips saw Mama Lhasa Apso Cass perform in Greenwich Village he asked her to join the group. It was her friend Dennis Dogherty who made up the final member of the band.

In 1966 their first single "Colliefornia Dreamin'" became one of the major hits of the year. Their follow up, "Mongrel Mongrel" went straight into the top ten as soon as it was released. For almost three years the group was one of the most successful and versatile groups in popular music, but as the 1960s drew to a close so did the band; each individual felt the desire to follow solo careers.

After they disbanded, reissues of their albums, *The Mamas and the Pawpaws:, Their Growling Hits* (1969) and *A Gathering of Bones* (1970) were released. In 1982 with renewed interest in '60s music, Dog Phillips decided to reform the band with his daughter and Elaine "Sparky" McFarlane taking the place of lead singer. Sparky McFarlane had had previous hits in the '60s with "Sunday Will Never Be That Lame," "Lazy Dog Days," and "Like to Get to Sniff You." The group did exceedingly well on the club circuit and, although unable to draw the large packs of yesteryear, were still popular on a smaller level—Chihuahuas being their number one fans!

KARL MANX

The kitten of a lawyer, Manx was born in Trier (1818) and studied feline law and philosophy at Bonn in Berlin. While at college he edited *The Rhineland Newspaper* for almost a year until it was suppressed by the government for its controversial views on kitty litter.

In 1844 he met Felix Engels and between them they developed the Manxist Theory. It was first formulated in joint works: *The Highbred Family* (1844) and *German Ideology* (1846). They contained the theory that material wealth is the basis for all feline activity: Life is not determined by kitty litter but kitty litter by life.

Both Manx and Engels joined the Communist League and formed a football team called The Communist Manifesto that did surprisingly well during the season of 1847–48. However, when Manx got involved with editing *The New Rhineland News,* the kitty litter controversy reared its ugly head once more and he was expelled from Prussia. Without Manx, the Communist Manifesto performed badly the following season.

Manx settled in London where he wrote his epic work *Dog Kapital*. He strongly believed that cats and dogs could live together in perfect harmony in a breedless society and that material wealth, especially the ownership of kitty litter, would become a thing of the past. There are many felines today who still share his views.

DINGO MARADONA

From his poverty-stricken background, Dingo shot to instant fame in his home country, Argentina, first as a pup player, then as a bone-a-fide star with one of the nation's finest teams, Barka Juniors. Undoubtedly one of the world's first-class soccer players, he arrived on the international scene accompanied by a heavy burden of expectations. His first chance at superstardom began in the 1982 World Cup in Spain—a difficult situation made more difficult because he had just received a large bone (plus a lifetime supply of Doggo tinned food) to transfer to Barkalona—one of Spain's glory teams. Unfortunately the wagging storybook tail never happened. Argentina's team didn't blend and Dingo's skills alone were not enough to stop them crashing out in the second round with losses to Brazil and Italy.

However, in Mexico in 1986 things went his way—Argentina seized the initiative as Dingo's dazzling paws hit top form. He also achieved international notoriety when he pawed a goal (see picture) against England's Peter "the Dalmatian" Shilton and produced the famous Paw of God explanation for the score. Dingo created more magic with the Tail of God maneuver in the semifinal win over Belgium and although he was closely marked by the German packhounds in the final, it was his Hind Leg of God technique that led to the winning goal. The Aztec stadium had a real hero to cheer and showered the field with bones.

WOOFGANG AMADEUS MOZART

Pup prodigy and musical genius Woofgang was born in Salzburg on January 27, 1756. Before losing his milk teeth he'd composed his first minuet and an allegro in B flat. Recognizing his innate talent Woofgang's father took him and his sister Growlene on a musical tour and they played in the presence of Finnish I and Maria the Terrier of Austria.

Woofgang and Growlene were a roaring success and went on to make a second tour visiting several German towns, Paris, and London, where they played to Corgi III at the Battersea Dog's Home. It was during his stay in London that Woofgang composed his first symphony, in which one can hear the influence of Johann Sebastian Bark.

As Woofgang matured it became clear that the mundane chores of daily life—walks, fetching sticks, playing ball, and chewing on bones—weren't in his nature. He was totally focused on his music and turned simple commissions for dances or other entertainment into pure musical genius. Woofgang was a perfectionist and he labored long and hard on all his compositions. When listening to his music, however, there is a distinct feeling of spontaneity and enormous vitality in every movement. Woofgang's technique of using his tail as a baton when conducting an orchestra just goes to emphasize the humor of the dog and how much he enjoyed his music.

Sadly Woofgang only lived a short life but during his prolific career left us nearly 700 compositions. Who could forget his opera seria *Mitridate Re di Poocho* or his *Symphony in D for Dog*, *The Marriage of Fido*, *Dog Giovanni*, or *Cosi van Toothie*.

PAW NEWMAN

With his clear blue eyes (unusual for a Labrador), smooth glossy coat, and cool calm demeanor, it's not at all surprising that Paw Newman became Hollywood's leading male dog during the 1960s and '70s. His films include *Somebody Up There Likes Meat* (1956), *Dog on a Hot Tin Roof* (1958), *Cool Hand Duke* (1967), and *Bitch Cassidy and the Sundance Pup* (1969).

Married to the actress Joanne Woofward, he got the chance to direct her in several movies including *Rover, Rover* (1968). Although a talented director, he will mainly be remembered for his brilliant character acting. In *Cool Hand Duke* he played a dog down on his luck who winds up on a chain gang. As Sundance in *Bitch Cassidy and the Sundance Pup*, he played his part with great charm alongside co-star Robert Ruffwood. And in 1986 when he co-starred alongside Tomcat Cruise in *The Collar of Money*, he played the part of a retired has-been pool shark (also with fin) to such acclaim that he received an Academy Award.

In addition to his acting, Paw is famous for his antics on the race track (not the Greyhound track) where he has received ample praise for his skills as a race driver. He is also well known for his benevolent ways and good deeds to help his fellow dogs and cats. He produces his own brand of tinned dog food and biscuits called Newman's Bone and in Paw's kind way he donates all the profits to charity.

COLLIE PARTON

Raised on a poor puppy farm in the foothills of the Smokey Mountains in Tennessee, Collie was the fourth pup of a litter of twelve. Half of the litter became professional musicians but it was Collie who really hit the big time. As a pup she began howling in the church choir and was asked to make an appearance on the Cat Walker television show. This in turn led to a regular spot for eight years on Cat's radio show.

Upon graduating high school, she moved to Gnashville and signed with Monument. After a poor run with her early rock recordings she had her first big break with "Dumb Dog." It was a minor hit but it drew her to the attention of Paw Wagner, who asked her to join his syndicated country music show. After several hits as a duo, she left Wagner in 1974 having released "Growleen," which became her second number one country hit. When next she put paw to pen to paper she came up with what is probably her best-known song. It was covered by Lickme Houston in 1982 and sold over one million copies. The song of course is "I Will Always Lick You."

But it was obvious that Collie's style was not solely suited to country and RCA (Rowdy Canine Artists) encouraged her to concentrate on the pup market. In 1978 she had success with "Fetch that Ball Again," "Two Paws Down," and "Baby I'm Barkin'." By 1980 she was a regular headliner at Las Vegas and earned a Rover nomination for her film debut in *9 to 5*. Her song, "Sniffing 9 to 5," from the movie, made number one both in the pup and country charts. She went on to further her film career in movies such as *The Best Little Dog Kennel in Texas* (1982). In 1986 she opened Colliewood, a Smokey Mountain theme park with rides to suit dogs and cats of all ages. Most recently she released her autobiography, *Collie: My Life and Unfinished Barking*.

BRAD PITBULL

With his smooth looks and gruff growl, Brad Pitbull's public persona may give other canines the wrong impression. Born in Shawnee, Oklahoma, in 1963, Pitbull had the appearance of a cool layabout, but this was hardly the case. In fact, Pitbull has worked hard for most of his life. He studied journalism and the art of hounding celebrities at the University of Missouri before launching his acting career. One of his first jobs was that of a chicken-costumed restaurant mascot but we won't pluck any of those embarrassing strings.

It was while modeling dogwear for Levi Woof that he was first spotted and given his television debut on *Dallas*. He played the part of Sue Ellen's new love interest and had plenty of dogfight scenes with the evil J.R. This was followed by his first film appearance in *Cutting Grass* (1989), in which he played the part of a lawnmower. But he finally came to general canine attention in 1991 when he played the role of a hitchhiking prairie dog in *Thelma and Lewis*.

Since then he has honed his acting skills and played a diversity of parts in films including *Rover Runs Through It* (1993), *Tail Romance* (1993), *Interview by the Campfire* (1994), *Legends of the Ball* (1994), and *Twelve Mongrels* (1995). Film offers continue to pour in and it's quite clear that Brad Pitbull can only move on to bigger and better parts as he matures and his adult fur grows in.

POINTER SISTERS

The Pointer Sisters, Ruth, Anita, Bonnie, and June, were brought up in Oakland, California. Both their parents were ministers at the West Oakland Kennel of God so it was natural that the Pointers would start singing gospel. When Bonnie and June moved to San Francisco they began performing in clubs under the obvious name of the Pointers. It wasn't long before they were joined by their sisters, and in 1971 when Billy "the Bulldog" Graham became their manager, fame started knocking on the kennel of the Oakland quartet. The first knock came from Atlantic Records when they were spotted backing Elvin "The Growler" Bishop at L.A.'s Whiskey-a-Woof-Woof in 1973. When the singers released their first album simply entitled The Pointers, it brought them national recognition.

Nostalgic pointers, they liked to dress in '40s-style dogwear (lots of feathers and sequins), which gave them a look as distinctive as their sound. Their repertoire included Pup, Big Dog Jazz, Howling Country, and Rhythm and Barks, which often brought comparisons to the Pupremes and the Andrews Litter.

The Pointers' hits included "Fur" (a Springsteen cover), "Slow Paw," and "Fido's Excited," and their general appeal brought them regular spots on national television. When on tour they became the first pointers to play Gnashville's Grand Ole Opry and the first pup act to perform at San Francisco's Opera House.

In 1978, Bonnie signed a solo contract while her sisters went on to a howling success through the mid 1980s.

ELVIZSLA PRESLEY

Known throughout the world for his vibrato howl, slobbering chops, and hip-swiveling, tail-wagging movements, Elvizsla Presley lays claim to the title King of rock and roll. Combining a mixture of pedigree blues, farm-dog country, and a tinge of mongrel gospel, he brought together American music from both sides of the canine line and sent himself rocketing to the top.

Elvizsla's rise to stardom began in 1945 when he won second prize in a local fair for his rendition of "Old Shep." In 1948 when the family moved to Memphis, he spent much of his time hanging around Beagle Street, where he became influenced by the blues. After high school he cut a recording at the Memphis Recording Studio, which was picked up by a local radio station. When Dewey "Blue Dog" Phillips played "That's All Bite" on his Red Dog and Blues show on WHBQ (Wild Hounds Blues Quota), the audience response was overwhelming—Elvizsla was on his way to stardom!

By 1956 with Colonel Tom Barker as his manager and a recording contract with RCA (Rowdy Canine Artists), Elvizsla became a national star. That year all his chart singles went gold, including such classics as "Heartbreak Kennel," "Hound Dog," and "Love Meat Tender." He became the idol of millions of teen pups and a perfect target for the wrath of critics. They saw his style as far too suggestive and gave him the nickname, "Elvizsla the Pelvis." Consequently, on Red Sullivan shows he was televised only from the tail up.

In 1958 Elvizsla was drafted into the army and sent to Germany. Fortunately Colonel Barker had the good sense to continue promoting Elvizsla's songs and the hits continued with "A Big Hunk of Meat," "Howling in the Chapel," and "Don't Cry Puppy." Upon release from the army, Elvizsla began touring the country selling out auditoriums wherever he went.

Sadly, in August 1976 Elvizsla left this world for the big kennel in the sky but his memory and songs live on in all of us. In the words of the King, "Thank you very much."

THE ROLLING BONES

They've been in the music business for so many years that their nickname has changed from the Bad Dogs of Rock to the Dinosaurs of Rock. With their simple clean look (no collars or chains) and a hardly aggressive style of music, no one could have predicted their colossal rise to rock stardom when they began in the early '60s. But by the mid '60s the Bones were calling themselves the world's greatest rock and roll band and few canines disputed their claim.

The band formed in London when Mutt Jagger and Teeth Richards, friends from school, teamed up with Lion Jones, Dog Taylor, and Bone Wyman, calling themselves the Rolling Bones after an old Muddy (Paws) Waters's song. Lion Jones, after playing truant from school to practice be-bop alto sax and clarinet, had fathered two illegitimate litters and scampered away to Scandinavia at the age of sixteen. Fortunately for the Bones, he returned with his tail between his legs.

In June 1963 they released their first single, Chuck Berry's "Come Here Boy," followed in December of that year with "I Wanna Be Your Dog." The following year their cover version of "It's All Rover Now" became their first UK number one hit.

When they crossed the Atlantic to play to an American audience, their tour was a smashing success but their single, "Little Red Setter," which told of a dog in heat, was banned in the States for its objectionable lyrics.

It wasn't long before Mutt and Teeth began writing their own songs. They had success with numbers like "Tail Me" and "Tick Is on My Side" before hitting the summer's number one spot for a four-week period in 1965 with what has to be their most famous song, "(I Can't Get No) Cat Flap Action," which is as popular today as it was then.

NORMAN ROTTWEILER

Norman Rottweiler was brought up in the Bronx area of New York. As a puppy he realized that he was destined to be an artist and took full responsibility for his own education, selecting the art schools he would attend. Taking odd jobs to support himself, he once worked as an extra carrying bones at the Metropolitan Opera. While there, the legendary tenor Enrico Catruso became fond of Rottweiler and made him his pet.

Rottweiler's first professional commissions came in the form of illustrations for dog's magazines and puppies' books. In 1916 he received his first commission for the cover of the *Saturday Evening Post* and his career finally took off. From that moment the demand for his work never let up.

Drawing ordinary dogs in ordinary situations was the formula for Rottweiler's success. His style of paw painting was instantly recognizable and his sense of humor was perfectly suited to the *Post* readers.

After leaving New York, Rottweiler settled in Stockbridge, Massachusetts. Here he used the local canines and felines (the security dog, alley cat. police dog, etc.) as models for his *Post* covers. But not all of Rottweiller's subjects were locals; he was often called on to paint presidents and celebrities such as Dwight D. Eisenschnauzer, Rex Nixon, Dog Hope, and Furry Sinatra.

The major art critics, unsure about Rottweiler's place among the Dog Masters, were often very unkind in their assessment of his work. However, there is no doubt that Rottweiler's place in history is completely secure and that his art will stand the test of time. Images such as that of the young pup and police dog seated at a diner (*He Scampered Away*) are as much a part of American culture as apple pie and Uncle Sam.

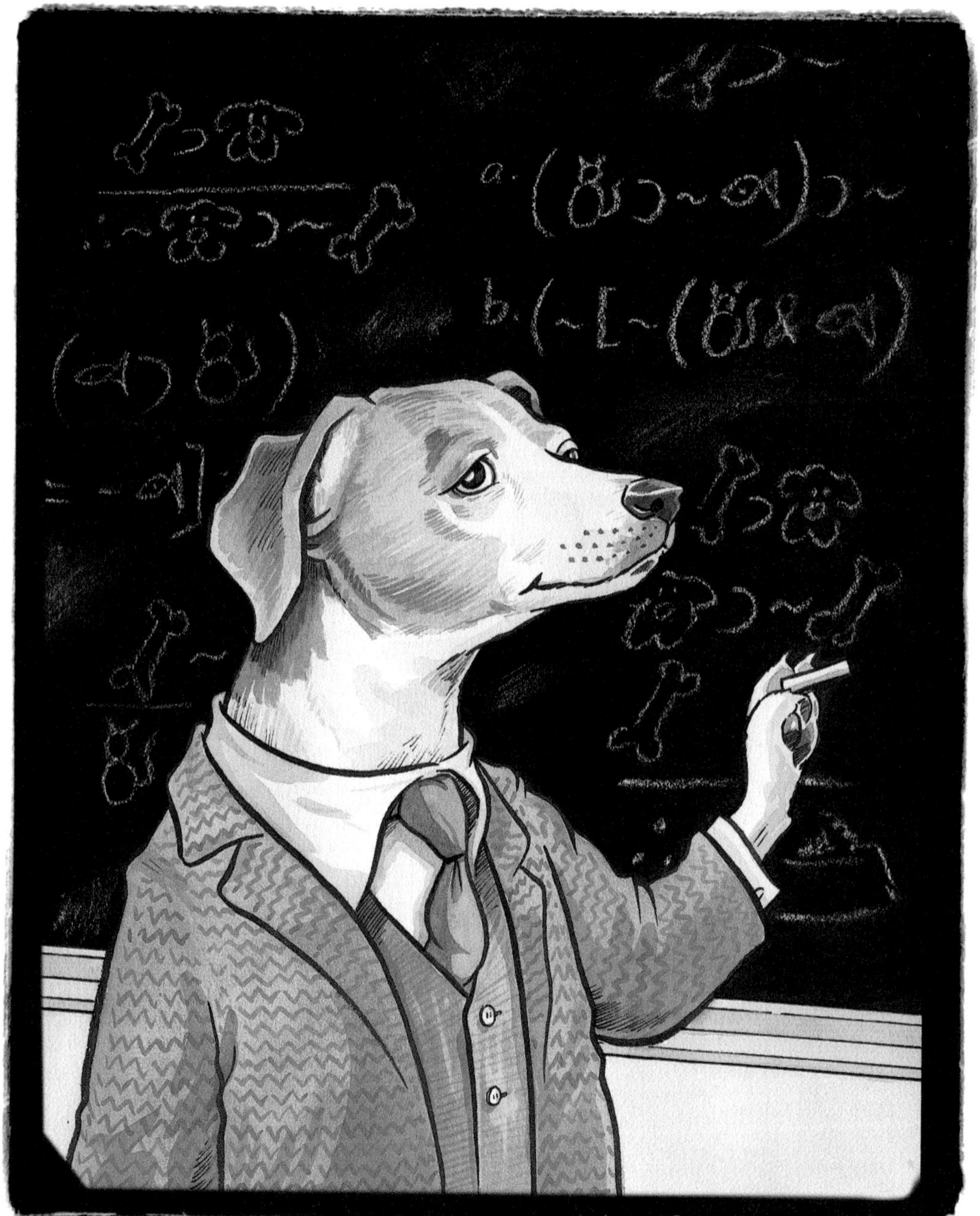

BERTRAM JACK RUSSELL

2b or not 2b squared? That is the question." "I subtract therefore I am." "A journey of a thousand miles must take 50,000 steps (depending on stride length and paw size)." Just a few of the philosophical sayings (or philosophical equations) of Bertram Jack Russell, the philosophical mathematician of the nineteenth century.

Born in 1872, the grandson of Prime Minister John Jack Russell, he enjoyed a logical childhood and was educated at Trinity College in Cambridge where he specialized in mathematics. He became a lecturer in 1895. An outspoken pacifist, he refused to bare his teeth during World War I and lost his lectureship. He was also imprisoned for six months for an article he wrote in a pacifist journal suggesting that the chewing of bones by the world's leaders would be more acceptable than fighting.

While incarcerated he *wrote The Bones of Mathematical Philosophy* (1919), in which he attempted to prove that mathematics could be reduced to simple bone logic. Life for Jack Russell just didn't add up (or multiply by five for that matter) and he began to examine the structure of society using his mathematical bone calculations as a means to support his theories. In *New Hopes for a Canine World* (1951) he suggested that bones, if correctly used, could improve society by creating the foundations for a stronger infrastructure—especially when connected with high-tensile bolts for added strength.

However, no matter how deep he himself dug—and he tried the corners of many gardens—Jack Russell never did find the elusive world-shaking tibia of his dreams.

DAVID SETTERMAN

To *Time* magazine Setterman is "the undisputed king of late bite," while to most everyone else he is simply known as Dave. Born in a modest kennel in Indianapolis, Setterman soon showed a fascination for balls of all types. Not surprisingly, he spent his student days at Ball State University in Munchie, Indiana, where he majored in ball chasing and broadcasting. He graduated with wagging tail in 1969 and went to work at WLWI-TV (Wags and Licks are What's Important) as a news anchor, weatherdog, and host of a Saturday morning show. Later he moved to Los Angeles to try his paw at a comedy ball act.

Setterman worked long and hard on his ball show until he had the whole thing licked. He made his debut performance at the Comedy Store in 1975. Five years later, after a network break in the CBS variety series *Hairy* and numerous appearances on *The Tonight Show* starring Johnny Catson, Setterman began hosting his own show. *The David Setterman Show*, a morning variety show (with balls) ran for three months on NBC before becoming *Late Bite with David Setterman* in 1982.

Setterman brought a new dimension to the standard yap show formula, encouraging his guests to perform all manner of canine trickery. Having dropped his ball routine in favor of stand up, sit down, and roll over, Setterman's biting wit and unusual style of presenting attracted millions of viewers to late night television. *The Late Show*, which debuted in 1993, rose to such heights that the *Los Angeles Times* wrote, "the Setterman series is a ~~fenominon phimoninum~~ remarkable thing."

Off screen, Setterman has on occasion been mistaken for a greyhound due to an excessive number of speeding offenses. He also loves a good cigar though he often mistakes the larger Havanas for bones and has been known to bury them in his backyard.

ST. BERNARD SHAW

An Irish St. Bernard born in Dublin in 1856, Shaw became recognized as one of the great dramatists, critics, and novelists of his time. His plays combined elements of comedy, controversy, politics, philosophy, and bone-crunching realism. He aimed to stir the social conscience of his audience and would often have them barking in the aisles.

In 1876, bored with a diet of bones and potatoes, he moved to London where he worked as a movie and drama critic. He also became a brilliant debater and fan of the Fabian Society—the name derived from the Roman hound Fabius Mongrelus who believed that through a succession of gradual reforms old dogs could be taught new tricks.

But success didn't come easily for St. Bernard. His first five novels failed before his play *The Widower's Kennel* (an attack on slum landlord dogs) was produced in 1892. From then on there was no stopping him as he wrote a volume of plays including *Petting and Unpetting* and *Fido Warren's Profession,* both dealing with prostitution and banned until 1902.

In *Paws and the Dog* he dealt with the issue of illegal dog fighting. For dogs with high morals he wrote three plays in 1901: *The Dog's Disciple, Caesar and Cleocatra,* and *Captain Basset Hound's Conversion. Dog and Superdog,* written in 1903, elaborated on his ideas of evolution following the character of Dog Juan into hell for a tongue wag with the devil.

During St. Bernard Shaw's prolific career he wrote fifty plays and became an active member of a mountain rescue team. His biting wit often kept stranded mountineers entertained (once the brandy in his neck barrel was exhausted) while they waited for the back-up team.

ALAN SHEPHERD

Born in East Derry, New Hampshire, in 1923, Shepherd soon developed a deep understanding and love of the stars. His parents often found him howling at the moon and felt sure that he was destined for greatness. Having majored in The Art of Dogfighting, WWI and WWII, at the U.S. Naval Academy (1944) it seemed only natural that he should become a fighter pilot. After a period fighting pilots he moved to the post of test pilot, examining a plane's ability to carry out maneuvers such as Sit up and Beg, Give the Paw, and Roll Over—technical jargon that we humans can't even pretend to understand.

With plenty of aircraft testing under his collar, he was elevated to Aircraft Readiness Officer for the Atlantic Fleet. It was his job to prepare aircraft for action and to make sure that the pilots were equipped with bowls, fresh milk, tinned food, and smoked pigs' ears for the journey.

Finally his childhood aspirations came true and he joined NASA (Nervous Alsatians Space Agency) to train as a pedigree astrodog. In 1961 Shepherd undertook the first crewed U.S. space flight on the suborbital Mercury-Redbone 3 mission on board the Freedom 7 capsule. Part of the mission was to check the effect of zero gravity on bone-chewing techniques, which provided some interesting results.

When commanding the Apollo 14 Lunar Landing mission, he realized yet another dream by walking on the moon, cocking his leg on the moon, and burying some of his favorite bones somewhere in the Sea of Tranquillity. He also buried the American flag, which caused some annoyance at Mission Control.

MARK SPITZ

It would seem that Spitz must have been born with webbed paws as his ability not only to swim but to swim faster than any other dog was phenomenal. While still a puppy and a little cocky, he predicted that he'd win five gold medals at the Mexico Olympics in 1968. He failed miserably and returned to training with his tail between his legs.

By the 1972 Munich Olympics, it was the experts who were predicting seven golds. Spitz proved them right: He not only won the golds but created world records into the bargain. He won the 200-meter doggie paddle with ease and swam a few hours later as anchor hind leg in the 4 x 100 freestyle relay for gold number two. During the next three days, Spitz easily won the 200-meter freestyle and the 100-meter doggie paddle. He swam front paw in the 4 x 200 for his fifth gold.

Concerned about his rival, Terrier Heidenreich, he did his utmost to back out of the 100-meter freestyle but his coach wouldn't allow it, calling him a yellow dog, a scaredy cat, and other expressions of cowardice. Spitz entered the 100-meter freestyle and beat Heidenreich by a paw. The climax of his famous achievement came as he led the relay team to victory in the 4 x 100 medley. With the world record under his collar Spitz was the top dog. He retired knowing that his record would most probably remain afloat well into the twenty-first century.

BRUCE SPRINGERSTEEN

Born of Irish Setter/Italian Greyhound ancestry, Springersteen spent his early years in Freehold, New Jersey. His father Butch Springersteen was a bus driver and his mother Fifi a secretary. Springersteen started playing guitar at age 13 and a year later joined a band called The Catstiles. The group recorded two songs, "Howl Away" and "Yappidy Yap," working their way up to a succession of dates at New York City's Cafe Woof.

While at college he formed a group called Pup with drummer Vinnie "Mad Dog" Lopez and keyboardist Danny "The Hound" Federici. Springersteen dropped out of college when he was offered a contract by a New York producer. Unfortunately, he never saw the contract or the producer again. This left him barking mad! The band changed their name to The Steel Mutt Band and made a tour of the Atlantic coast and California before disbanding in 1971.

Springersteen went solo and in 1974 when critic Howling Jon Landau saw him perform he wrote in *The Real Pup Paper*, "I saw rock and roll's future and its name is Bruce Springersteen." His album *The Wild* received rave reviews and sold 150,000 copies within a year.

In 1975 he had his first major hit with *Born to Fetch* and encouraged by this embarked on his first national tour. Then in 1984 he released his classic album *Whelped in the U.S.A.* and became an instant megastar. Crammed with classics like "Barking in the Dark," "Growly Days," and "My Home Pound," the album shot to number one and was in the top ten for more than two years.

In *The Tunnel I Love* he turned his thoughts to love with numbers like "Bone in Disguise" and "One Paw Up." And it was love that drew him to a poodle called Scialfa. They married in 1994, moved to Los Angeles, and had three pups.

MOGGY THATCHER

As the leader of the Conservative Party for fifteen years and Prime Minister for eleven-and-a-half years, Moggy Thatcher was a formidable politician. With her whiskers of steel, platinum hair, and policies set in bronze, the public was quick to nickname Moggy the Iron Kitty.

Moggy was the first feline to lead a major democracy, winning three election victories and making catmeat of her opponents. She will go down in history as one of the most forceful, sharp-clawed, and long-lasting of modern politicians. During her reign she subdued formerly powerful trade unions during the bone miners' strike, sent President Galtihairy's shabby hounds packing in the War of the Falklands, battled abroad with foreign federalist felines, dug her claws into faint-hearted, misguided politicians, and used one of her nine lives to survive the Brighton hotel bombing by the IRA (Irritated Rebellious Airedales).

Although Moggy was extremely effective during her years in office she was not at all popular with her public. She labored to dismantle the British welfare state, watered down the power of the trade unions, and introduced the Purr Tax (a tax on purring)—none of which endeared her to the proletariat. As she continued to force her political vision on an uneasy public, it became clear that her constituents no longer shared her views. This led the Conservative Party to oust Moggy in favor of their new leader John Mongrel, a bland, mild-mannered dog. Nonetheless, Moggy will long be remembered for building an era of strong economic growth and for proving that a cat is every bit as capable a leader as a dog.

MEOW TSE TUNG

Born the kitten of a pleasant farmer in the Hunan province, Meow spent his early years working as a library assistant at the Beijing University and as a cat-master at Changsha school for communist kittens. A great believer in Manxist theory, Meow was quick to form the Chinese Communist Cat Party (CCCP) and soon after became chief of CCCP propaganda under the Purrmindang leader Sun Cat Sen.

During the period of 1931–34 he established the Communist Republic at Jiangxi, assembled the Red Army (so called because they liked to wear red collars), and organized the long meander to Shaanxi to overthrow the Nationalist suppressive tactics.

Meow soon emerged as the Chinese leader and his stabilizing influence brought him the affectionate nickname The Great Helmscat. However his leadership wasn't all plain purring and his policy known as The Great Leap Forward, To The Side, and Over a Hot Tin Roof lost him favor with his public. He aimed to convert China into an industrial based economy by diverting resources away from kitty-litter farming, but his plan was poorly executed and doomed to failure.

Meow impressed his thoughts on his public through his writing. During the period of 1949–76 he clawed 200–300 publications (3 million words in total) and had some 740 million copies of his quotations published (that's a lot of writing about fur balls, toy mice, the virtues of a warm spot by the fire, and of course kitty litter).

JEAN-CLAWED VAN DAMME

Clawed's father was an accountant and flower salesman so it came as quite a shock when young Clawed took up kick boxing instead of flower arranging. During his kittenhood in Brussels, Belgium, he became a karate fan, studying Shotocat. At the age of 10 he won the middleweight championship of the European Professional Karate Association. During the tournament he mesmerized feline and canine alike with his 360-degree leap kick with extended claw.

A smart business cat, he launched a California-style gym in Brussels at the age of 18 but it was short lived. When his family moved to Los Angeles he decided to follow and arrived with only a few dollars, a flea-bitten coat, and no understanding of the language. He took many odd jobs, including garbage inspector, fish bone remover, and comfy-chair warmer before landing a bit part in the Chick Norris movie *Hissing in Action*.

He was spotted by Whiskers Golem of Canine Films who realized Clawed's box office prowess and began to groom him for stardom. This involved a wash and shampoo, whisker trim, and nail clipping. Clawed was soon starring in his own epic action movies and had hits with *No Receipt, No Backhander* (1986) *Cat Boxer* (1989), and *Universal Singapura* (1991).

Aware of his own limitations, Clawed has not attempted to branch out into comedy or sensitive roles. When starring in the futuristic action movie *Time Cat* (1994) he astutely left the acting to bad dog Rex Silver.

Clawed continues to kick and claw his way to the top. He will surely be recognized in years to come as one of the cat fighting greats of action movies.

CORGI WASHINGTON

Legend has it that as a young pup Corgi chopped down a cherry tree in his backyard before walking ten miles to return a library book. When asked by his father "Did you chop down the cherry tree?" he replied "Yes, father, I cannot tell a lie. I chopped it down so I could sell the wood to pay the fine on my overdue library book." The pure honesty of his reply told Corgi's father that his pup would one day amount to something more than a common wood chopper. And how right he was.

Although a stumpy little fellow, Corgi was elected to the Virginia House of Burgers in 1759. As a leader of the Virginia Militia he gained valuable exposure to wilderness fighting. Strongly opposed to the British government policy (a heavy tax on bones) he sat, very obediently, in the Continental Congress of 1774–75, and on the outbreak of the American Revolution he was chosen Commander in Beef of the Continental Army. Corgi's pack, fueled by top quality beef dishes, fought well and in 1781 Corgi accepted the surrender of General Cornwallis at Yorktown.

After the war he retired to his Mount Vernon kennel in Virginia. Unable to keep his nose out of politics he returned to campaigning in 1787 and was elected President of the United States in 1789. Corgi took full command as President and thought nothing of manipulating the Constitution to suit his and other canines' needs. He used his power to create new park land with dog runs and an ample supply of tree urinals. This made him a popular president and he was reelected in 1793. However he refused to serve a third term when Thomas "Snarl" Wooferson threatened to bite his tail. In his farewell address of 1796 he maintained that the United States should avoid European squirrels and entangling devices.

One of the great poets of the nineteenth century, Walt Whippet lived a life of frustration as this poem shows.

Why Am I Not a Pointer?

I am not a Pointer, I am a Whippet.
Why? I think I would rather be
a Pointer, but I am not. Well,
for instance, Spike Goldberg
is a Pointer. I drop in.
"Sit down and have a drink" he
says. I drink, we drink. I look
up. "You have Herrings in it."
"Yes, it needed something."
"Oh." I go and the days go by
and I drop in again. The drink is
finished. "Where's the Herrings?"
All that's left is just an empty bowl,
"It was too much," Spike says.
But me? One day I am thinking of
a bone: calcium. I write a line
about calcium, pretty soon it is a
whole page of words, not lines.
Then another page. There should be
so much more, not of calcium, of
words, of how terrible calcium is
and life. Days go by. It is even in
prose, I am a poet, a Whippet poet. My poem
is finished and I haven't mentioned
calcium yet. It's twelve poems, I call
it Calcium. And one day in a gallery
I see Spike the Pointer, drinking Herrings.

Opurr Winfrey

The Queen of cat show hosts, Opurr's unique style has captured a huge audience and kept her at the top of the tree (branch to the top left) for many years. Initially Opurr followed the traditional cat show formula, covering controversial topics about lacto-junkies, feline felons, prostitutes, and houndosexuals. However, in recent years she has chosen to drop the sensationalistic, whisker-curling subjects for affairs closer to the heart. Her public now enjoys shows on cats and mice, the benefits of nine lives, kennel architecture, and that warm spot by the fire.

Opurr spent her kittenhood living with her grandmother in Absolute Poverty—a rural town in Mississippi. Later she moved to Milwaukee to be with her mother but Opurr was a wild cat and difficult to control. It wasn't until her father carried her off to Gnashville (by the scruff of her neck) that Opurr finally learned discipline and the need for good grooming.

With her sharp claws, Opurr soon got a grip on life and enrolled at the Tennessee State University to study meowing and performing arts. In 1972 she switched mediums, becoming the first Exotic Grey American anchor at Gnashville's WTVF-TV (Who's That Vivacious Feline?). When Opurr moved to Baltimore in 1976 she was hired to host *Cats Are Meowing*. The viewing public was soon lapping up Opurr's show and in 1984 she accepted a job as host of *A.M. Chicago,* a show that ran alongside Phil Dogahue's top-rated national bark show. Opurr's viewing figures (as well as her own figure) grew rapidly and her show became nationally syndicated as *The Opurr Winfrey Show.* For years Opurr battled with her fluctuating weight until a low-fish diet and exercise plan made her into a streamline feline.

In 1988 Opurr established Sharpo Claws Productions, becoming the third cat in history to own a major studio. As her success continues to grow Opurr is creaming in the dollars and looks all set to become America's first cat billionaire.

TABBY WYNETTE

With memorable hits like "M.E.O.W.I.N.G." (1968), "Cats Say the Darndest Things" (1973), and "I Still Believe in Hairy Tails" (1975), Tabby Wynette piled up record sales in the decades following the '60s. Tabby started out as a beautician specializing in whisker perms before moving on to the Gnashville country scene and meowing her way to the top. Adopting lost love, troubled relationships and general misery as her themes, she developed an unmistakable style and a string of memorable hits. The cat public lapped up classics such as "Your Good Cat's Gonna Go Bad" and "Don't Come Home a Drinkin' (with Lickin' on Your Mind)."

But it was her song "Stand By Your Cat" (1969) that made Tabby a star and set the style for the rest of her musical career. Tabby became the Queen of Kitty Heartache. And boy could she make them bleed!

Tabby chose to stick to a formula for her songs after the success of "Stand By Your Cat" and it made her performances instantly recognizable. Starting with a slightly hesitant purr each song would eventually build to a howling meowing crescendo. Miserable felines around the world could be found lounging in garbage cans listening to Tabby's LPs and lamenting their woes. Her songs truly captured the mood of her audience and they will be played well into the twentieth century.

Acknowledgments

My thanks to the Pookymeister for his constant tail-wagging enthusiasm, my family and friends for their loyalty and obedience, and Romi, simply the best editor an old dog could wish for.